W9-ASC-110

921
HEN
c l

Worth, Richard
King Henry VIII and the
Reformation. . .

DATE DUE	BORROWER'S NAME

921
HEN

Worth, Richard
King Henry VIII and the
Reformation. . .

Morrill School Library
Chicago Public Schools
6011 S. Rockwell
Chicago, IL 60629

KING HENRY VIII
and the Reformation
in World History

Titles *in World History*

**Captain Cook Explores
the Pacific
in World History**
0-7660-1823-7

**Christopher Columbus
and the
Age of Exploration
in World History**
0-7660-1820-2

**Cinqué of the *Amistad*
and the Slave Trade
in World History**
0-7660-1460-6

**Commodore Perry Opens
Japan to Trade
in World History**
0-7660-1462-2

**Cortés and the Conquest
of the Aztec Empire in
World History**
0-7660-1395-2

**Hernando de Soto
and the Spanish
Search for Gold
in World History**
0-7660-1821-0

**Julius Caesar and
Ancient Rome
in World History**
0-7660-1461-4

**King Henry VIII
and the Reformation
in World History**
0-7660-1615-3

**King Richard
the Lionhearted
and the Crusades
in World History**
0-7660-1459-2

**Lenin and the
Russian Revolution
in World History**
0-7660-1464-9

**Leonardo da Vinci and
the Renaissance
in World History**
0-7660-1401-0

**Mahatma Gandhi and
India's Independence
in World History**
0-7660-1398-7

**Nelson Mandela and
Apartheid in
World History**
0-7660-1463-0

**Philip II and Alexander
the Great Unify Greece in
World History**
0-7660-1399-5

**Pizarro and the Conquest
of the Incan Empire in
World History**
0-7660-1396-0

**Robespierre and the
French Revolution
in World History**
0-7660-1397-9

**Stanley and Livingstone
and the Exploration of
Africa in World History**
0-7660-1400-2

KING HENRY VIII
and the Reformation
in World History

Richard Worth

Enslow Publishers, Inc.

40 Industrial Road   PO Box 38
Box 398   Aldershot
Berkeley Heights, NJ 07922   Hants GU12 6BP
USA   UK

http://www.enslow.com

C 1   2003   18.85

Library of Congress Cataloging-in-Publication Data

Worth, Richard.
  King Henry VIII and the Protestant Reformation in world history /
  Richard Worth.
       p. cm. — (In world history)
    Includes bibliographical references and index.
    ISBN 0-7660-1615-3
     1. Henry VIII, King of England, 1491–1547—Juvenile literature.
  2. Great Britain—History—Henry VIII, 1509–1547—Juvenile literature.
  3. Great Britain—Kings and rulers—Biography—Juvenile literature.
  4. England—Church history—16th century—Juvenile literature.
  5. Reformation—England—Juvenile literature. [1. Henry VIII, King of
  England, 1491–1547. 2. Great Britain—History—Henry VIII, 1509–1547.
  3. Reformation. 4. Kings, queens, rulers, etc.] I. Title. II. Series.
  DA332 .W67   2001
  942.05'2'092—dc21
                                        00-011833

Printed in the United States of America

10 9 8 7 6 5 4 3 2 1

To Our Readers: We have done our best to make sure all Internet addresses in this
book were active and appropriate when we went to press. However, the author
and the publisher have no control over and assume no liability for the material
available on those Internet sites or on other Web sites they may link to. Any
comments or suggestions can be sent by e-mail to comments@enslow.com or to
the address on the back cover.

Illustration Credits: Enslow Publishers, Inc., pp. 6, 12, 61; Library of
Congress, pp. 10, 19, 21, 23, 24, 41, 47, 63, 65, 71, 74, 79, 84, 89, 91, 96,
100, 102.

Cover Illustration: Library of Congress (Henry VIII portrait); © Digital
Vision Ltd. (Background).

Every effort has been made to locate the copyright owners of the pictures used in
this book. If due acknowledgment has not been made, we sincerely regret the
omission.

Contents

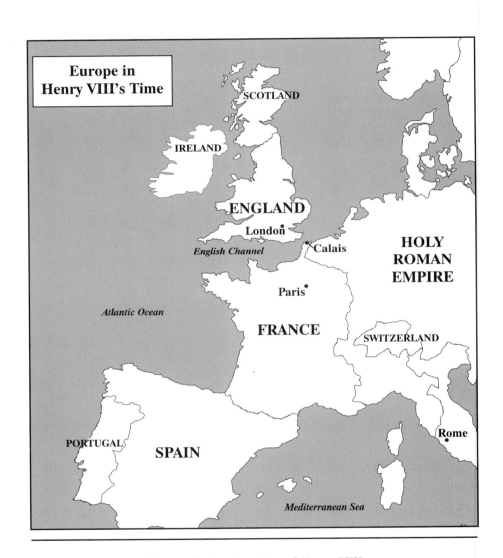

Europe during the reign of Henry VIII.

Chapter 1

King Henry's New Queen

In May 1533, a magnificent procession of three hundred barges floated down the river Thames on its way to London. On the barges sat richly clad aristocrats, court musicians, and government officials. At the center of the procession was the woman with whom the king, Henry VIII, had fallen deeply in love—the new queen of England, Anne Boleyn. She sat on a barge that had previously belonged to the former queen, Catherine.

King Henry VIII had decided to divorce Queen Catherine when she could not produce a male heir to the throne. Henry's dynasty, the Tudors, was only half a century old. (A dynasty is a line of rulers who come from the same family, or house.) The king feared that, without a male heir, he and his dynasty might be overthrown, plunging England into civil war. Internal strife had existed throughout the past century. Indeed, the king's father, Henry VII, had only taken control of the kingdom after winning it on the battlefield.

When the procession reached London, the courtiers who attended the queen marched along the streets. Queen Anne was carried on a litter made out of shimmering white cloth with silver bells hanging from the canopy over her head. Choirs sang to her as she went along the city streets. Houses and shops were hung with rich tapestries in honor of her arrival. The queen was dressed in white robes trimmed with fur, and on her head sat a crown of expensive jewels.

Usually, the coronation of a new queen was greeted with shouts of joy from the people of London. But this time, no one shouted the traditional "God Save the Queen!" Nor did many people tip their hats to the new queen. The majority of Londoners did not like Anne. They believed that Catherine was their rightful queen and that Anne had no right to sit on the throne beside King Henry.

The king had gambled on taking a new queen. He hoped Anne would give him the son and heir he so desperately wanted, to ensure peace and keep his dynasty from being overthrown. But in divorcing Catherine, Henry had been forced to renounce the Roman Catholic Church, which had refused to allow the divorce. In the process, he had dramatically transformed the Church in England. The king had sparked a reformation that would change his realm forever.

Chapter 2

England in Turmoil

In his play, *The Tragedy of Richard the Second*, English dramatist William Shakespeare described a king who was overthrown by powerful nobles who had grown unhappy with the king's dictatorial rule. As Richard was about to lose his crown, he speaks the lines:

> *What must the King do now? Must he submit?*
> *The King shall do it. Must he be depos'd?*
> *The King shall be contented. Must he lose*
> *The name of king? God's name, let it go.*[1]

The overthrow of Richard II in 1399 began almost a century of political turmoil in England. Richard had become king in 1377 while he was just a boy of ten. Many of the powerful lords in England considered him a weak ruler surrounded by misguided advisors.

Richard II on the throne in England, from an ancient painting in Westminster Abbey.

These lords controlled England's large estates—the major form of wealth—and the poor peasants tilled the land for them. Eventually, some of the great landowners rose up against Richard II, defeated the king in battle, and executed his chief advisors. At first, the king was allowed to stay on the throne, but he could do nothing. As he grew older, Richard improved as a leader. He increased his power and built up his own personal army. Finally, he struck back at the powerful landowners who had humiliated him, putting them behind bars and cutting off their heads. In 1399, when the Duke of Lancaster, a great landowner and heir to the throne, died, Richard seized the duke's lands and prevented them from being inherited by his eldest son, Henry of Bolingbroke. This was too much for Henry. He led an army of great nobles to overthrow Richard in 1399 and seize the throne for himself.

This new king, Henry IV, began the royal Lancastrian dynasty. During the early years of his reign, Henry was forced to deal with a series of revolts led by supporters of Richard as well as some of England's leading noble families. They were jealous of the king's power and wanted to replace him with someone they could control. Although Henry was successful in battle, the constant campaigning seemed to wear him out. He died in 1413, when he was in his forties.

Henry IV was succeeded by his son, also named Henry. Henry V was a young, handsome ruler who had helped his father triumph on the battlefield. During the early 1400s, besides fighting over the crown, England was at war with France. The English kings claimed the throne of France for themselves. Since 1345, they had been engaged in the Hundred Years' War for control of French territory. In 1415, Henry V won a decisive battle against the French at Agincourt, near the coast of France. According to one historian, "Henry emerged, still a young man, the most famous ruler in Europe."[2] He marched on Paris, the French capital, and married Catherine of Valois, daughter of the French king. Henry now controlled France, although most of this territory would be lost under his son's rule. The English people rejoiced in the great victory he had given them over their old enemies. He had united England in support of his monarchy.

The Reign of Henry VI

King Henry V remained on the throne only a few more years. At the age of thirty-five, he died in 1422, during one of his military campaigns. He left the

ENGLAND

English Channel

AGINCOURT

HOLY
ROMAN
EMPIRE

NORMANDY

Paris●

BRITTANY

CHAMPAGNE

ORLEANS

*Atlantic
Ocean*

POITOU

Lands held by England

Lands held by France

**Lands held by
duke of Burgundy**

**Lands recognizing
Henry VI of England**

Battle

BOURBON

AQUITAINE

SAVOY

AUVERGNE

GASCONY

DAUPHINE

ARMAGNAC

LANGUEDOC

PROVENCE

100 Years'
War

Mediterranean Sea

*England and France fought the Hundred Years' War over control of
certain areas of present-day France.*

country in the hands of his son, an infant barely nine months old who became Henry VI. Once again, England found itself without a powerful monarch.

At first, the child king was dominated by strong advisors who ruled England for him. When he finally became old enough to rule for himself, Henry's reign was plagued by another problem: The king suffered from mental illness. In 1453, he went temporarily insane. The English government was taken over by one of the king's main advisors, Richard, Duke of York, England's greatest landowner. However, York's power was strongly opposed by the king's wife, Margaret, and her supporters. The following year, when the king recovered his sanity, the Duke of York was forced from power.

Nevertheless, York refused to accept this situation. Leading an army of his own, the Duke of York defeated Henry and his followers at the Battle of St. Albans in 1455. This is usually considered the first battle in an English civil war known as the War of the Roses. The white rose was the symbol of York and the red rose became the symbol of Lancaster, Henry's dynasty.

The Duke of York took control of the government as a result of his victory at St. Albans, although Henry actually remained on the throne. Several years later, the Lancastrians seized the initiative. Their armies defeated the Yorkists, and the Duke of York was killed. However, his son, Edward of March, quickly avenged this defeat with two victories. King Henry VI fled from London. In 1461, Edward became king, as

Edward IV. The House of York was now supreme in England.

Edward IV and the Tudors

One of the strongest supporters of King Henry VI had been Jasper Tudor, Earl of Pembroke. The Tudor family came originally from Wales. During the thirteenth century, Ednyfed Fychan, a courtier to princes, received large grants of land for his services. He married a woman named Gwenllian and they had two sons, one of whom was named Tudur.

During the fourteenth century, the family continued to be large landowners in Wales. In the fifteenth century, Owen Tudor (the spelling of their name had changed) became a courtier to Catherine of Valois, the wife of Henry V and mother of Henry VI.

Several years after Henry V's death, Owen Tudor and Catherine were married. They had three sons—Edmund, Jasper, and Owen. Edmund and Jasper became nobles by the order of their half brother, King Henry VI. As king, he had the power to make anyone he wanted a lord of England. In 1455, Edmund married Margaret Beaufort, the great-great-granddaughter of King Edward III, who had ruled England during part of the fourteenth century. Although Edmund died a year later, his wife, Margaret, gave birth to a son soon afterward. His name was Henry Tudor.

With the death of Edmund, Henry Tudor was brought up by his mother and uncle Jasper. But, in 1460, after the Lancastrians were defeated, Tudor fortunes took a turn for the worse. Owen, Jasper's father, was captured and executed by the Yorkists. Pembroke Castle, where Henry Tudor was being raised, was attacked by armies loyal to the House of York. The castle was eventually forced to surrender.

Jasper escaped with his life. However, Henry was taken from his mother and put under the care of a loyal Yorkist family in Wales. He was a possible heir to the throne of England, and the Yorkists wanted to make sure he did not try to claim the kingdom.

During the 1460s, while Edward IV was king, Jasper hid from the authorities. He conducted a hit-and-run campaign with a few men under his command against Yorkist strongholds in Wales, Scotland, and Ireland. Suddenly, in 1470, Jasper's fortunes improved. Margaret, the wife of Henry VI, recaptured the throne for her husband with the help of the Earl of Warwick and his powerful army. Jasper was reinstated as an earl. He was powerful enough to rescue his nephew Henry Tudor from captivity and take him to London to meet Edward IV.

But Henry VI's days as king proved to be very short. Edward VI mounted a new campaign against the Lancastrians. He defeated them in two battles—at Barnet and at Tewkesbury in central England—in 1471. The Earl of Warwick was killed at Barnet. Henry VI was captured and sent to the Tower of London, a huge stone fortress where political prisoners were often held. Soon afterward, he was executed. Jasper and his nephew Henry Tudor fled England to live in Brittany, France. Here, they found safety with a local duke who was a friend of the Lancastrians. Henry, who had royal blood in his veins, was now the last male Lancastrian who could be considered an heir to the throne of England. But as long as Edward IV sat on the throne, there could be little chance that Henry would ever become king.

Richard III and Bosworth Field

After 1470, Edward IV brought a stable government to England. One of the king's strongest supporters was his brother, Richard, the Duke of Gloucester. Richard had fought at the battles of Barnet and Tewkesbury. Edward IV had also put him in charge of governing the northern part of England and defending the border against the independent kingdom of Scotland, which had been in conflict with the English kings for centuries. In addition, Richard headed the government in the large northern city of York, bringing it many years of sound administration.

In 1483, Edward IV died. He was succeeded by his son, twelve-year-old Edward V. However, young Edward's uncle Richard had decided that Edward was not suited to be king. England needed the firm hand of a proven warrior and administrator. No sooner was Edward declared king, than Richard headed for London with some of the powerful nobles, including the Duke of Buckingham.

Richard and his supporters seized Edward and his brother Richard, who were under the protection of their mother, Elizabeth Woodville. Richard then put them in the Tower of London. Richard declared that the young king was the illegitimate son of Edward IV, and therefore, not entitled to rule. Instead, the Duke of Gloucester took the throne as Richard III. Once young Edward and his brother entered the Tower, they were never seen again. Although there was no direct proof, many observers at the time believed that Richard had ordered them to be killed. In addition, he also executed some of the young king's chief advisors. As a result, many people in England grew fearful that Richard was a dictator who might kill anyone who stood in his way.

Some of the powerful nobles, including the Duke of Buckingham, decided that they could no longer remain loyal to Richard III. Instead, they threw their support to Henry Tudor, who was still living in France, as the true king of England.

In 1483, Buckingham led a revolt against Richard III. Henry Tudor arrived on English soil from Brittany with a small force to support the uprising. But the revolt was unsuccessful. Buckingham was caught and executed. Henry sailed back to France.

Once he had returned to France, he journeyed to the giant cathedral at Rennes. There, on Christmas Day, 1483, he swore an oath to marry Elizabeth, the oldest daughter of King Edward IV, and unite the dynasties of York and Lancaster after he became king.

Over the next eighteen months, dissatisfaction with Richard's rule continued to grow. In August 1485,

17

Henry and his uncle Jasper decided to lead another revolt against Richard III. The two men, with their army of about two thousand, landed in Wales and began to advance toward London. Although Henry picked up additional troops who had deserted the king, his forces were still outnumbered about two to one by the soldiers of King Richard III. Henry hoped to have the support of two powerful barons, Thomas and William Stanley. But the Stanleys told him they were not prepared to commit their forces to either side. Instead, they planned to stand by and wait to see who would gain the upper hand so they could be on the winning side.

The armies of Richard III and Henry Tudor clashed at Bosworth Field in central England on August 22, 1485. The battle seesawed back and forth, with knights on both sides being brutally killed as they lashed at each other with their spears and broadswords. But neither side could claim victory. Eventually, King Richard decided to take decisive action. With his small bodyguard, he charged toward Henry, who had taken a position on the battlefield next to the Tudor flag. At first, Richard's daring action seemed to be successful— some of Henry's knights were killed. At just this moment, however, the Stanleys decided to enter the battle on the side of Henry Tudor. Richard was sur-rounded. In William Shakespeare's play *The Tragedy of Richard the Third*, the king cries out: "A horse! A horse! My kingdom for a horse!"[3] But the king could not find a horse, and he was killed. Later, someone

Richard III (seen here) was finally defeated by Henry Tudor in the historic Battle of Bosworth Field.

found Richard's crown on the battlefield and handed it to Henry. A new king and a new royal house had come to England—Henry VII and the House of Tudor.

The Reign of Henry VII

When Henry became king in 1485, England had suffered from almost a century of civil war. In an effort to bring peace, the king surrounded himself with a mix of political advisors, some of whom had worked for the Yorkist kings, Richard III and Edward IV. Henry also carried out his pledge and married Edward's daughter, Elizabeth. In 1486, the queen gave birth to a child named Arthur. In him, the roses of York and Lancaster were combined into a third rose—the Tudor rose. A song written at the time went:

> *I love the rose both red and white.*
> *Is that your pure perfect appetite?*
> *To hear talk of them is my delight!*
> *Joyed may we be,*
> *Our prince to see,*
> *And roses three!*[4]

But the celebrations that followed the birth of an heir to the throne could not hide the fact that deep political divisions still existed. In 1487, for example, Henry VII faced a Yorkist uprising led by a man named Lambert Simnel, who claimed that he was the nephew of Edward IV and the rightful king of England. Although Simnel was a fake, he had the support of powerful barons who did not support Henry and wanted to put someone else on the throne whom they could control. The king gathered a strong army, and with the help of his uncle Jasper, he defeated Simnel, ending the uprising. Eight years later, the king faced another revolt, led by Perkin Warbeck, who claimed to be one of the princes who had been put in the Tower of London during the reign of Richard III. Warbeck also won the allegiance of some of the nobility who felt no loyalty to Henry. However, his revolt, too, was unsuccessful. Warbeck was captured by King Henry's supporters and hanged in 1499.

While he was dealing with these revolts, King Henry VII also tried to strengthen the central government in England to prevent more turmoil in the future. For example, he increased the number of justices of the peace. These officials were responsible for holding trials of people accused of crime. The justices were carefully supervised by the king's council of advisors and tied closely to the central administration in London, the nation's capital. Henry also wrote laws ordering the powerful barons not

Henry VII brought stability back to England and worked hard to protect the dynasty he had created.

21

to form their own private armies, like those that had caused such havoc during the War of the Roses. In addition, the king created a special court, called the Star Chamber. It met in a room that had stars on the walls. The Star Chamber tried powerful nobles who took justice into their own hands. These nobles might persecute anyone against whom they had a grudge, creating turmoil throughout the countryside. The Star Chamber brought them to justice and enforced the king's laws.

Another way that Henry hoped to strengthen the monarchy was to form alliances between the House of Tudor and other great monarchs of Europe. Among these were Ferdinand and Isabella, the king and queen of Spain. Monarchs have traditionally tried to create political alliances through marriage, just as Henry had married Elizabeth to unite the houses of York and Lancaster. During the 1490s, Henry made an agreement with Ferdinand and Isabella for Arthur, heir to the English throne, to marry their youngest daughter, Catherine of Aragon.

In 1501, fifteen-year-old Catherine arrived in England with a large group of courtiers who rode down the streets of London. As people hung out their windows to catch a glimpse of the heavily veiled young bride, she journeyed to St. Paul's Cathedral. In a ceremony that lasted over three hours, Catherine and Arthur were married by the Archbishop of Canterbury, England's highest-ranking priest in the Catholic Church. After the ceremony, shouts rang out

Ferdinand (left) and Isabella (right) of Spain were powerful rulers. Henry VII realized it would help him protect his throne if he allied with them through marriage.

at St. Paul's for Prince Arthur and his father, King Henry VII.

Henry Becomes Heir to the Throne

Before the marriage ceremony, Catherine had been led down the aisle at St. Paul's by Arthur's younger brother, Henry. Born in 1492, Henry was a round-faced, powerfully built boy with red hair. As the younger son of the king, he was not considered as important as his brother, who would one day inherit the throne. Nevertheless, Henry was given a broad education, supervised by his grandmother Margaret

As a second son, it seemed unlikely that Henry (seen here as a child) would someday become king. In fact, he would become one of the most important leaders in England's history.

Beaufort. Although most people in this period could neither read nor write, Beaufort was a very learned woman. Henry was her favorite grandson, and she wanted him to follow in her footsteps. As one observer at court put it:

> He mastered Latin and French, understood Italian . . .
> theology and mathematics, [and] displayed even in his
> boyhood that taste . . . in music which eventually made
> him an excellent performer on the organ, the lute and
> the harpsichord, as well as a composer. . . .[5]

As he grew, Henry learned to ride a horse, shoot arrows with a powerful longbow, and play tennis, which became one of his favorite sports. He also took part in tournaments, dressing in a full suit of armor and jousting with a long lance against other knights. Many observers regarded him as a true Renaissance prince, which meant that he excelled in a wide variety of areas.

In 1502, Henry also became something more—the heir to the English throne. His brother, Arthur, developed a serious illness, possibly dysentery—a disease of the intestine. At fifteen, Arthur died suddenly. Both his parents were greatly saddened by Arthur's death, but now their focus turned to his younger brother, Henry. Only a son could provide stability for England and ensure that the Tudor monarchy would continue. After all, the Tudor reign was only seventeen years old and was not yet firmly established. The Tudors might easily be overthrown, just as they had unseated Richard III.

Henry began to be trained by his father to take over the role of king. "It is quite wonderful how much the king likes the prince," reported Spanish Ambassador Hernán Duque. "He has good reason to do so, for the prince deserves all love. But it is not only from love that the king takes the prince with him; he wishes to improve him."[6]

Henry learned that the king had not only created a strong central government to pass on to his son, but he had also improved the financial strength of the monarchy. The War of the Roses had been very expensive for English monarchs. Henry VII brought relative peace to England, which reduced the amount of money that had to be spent paying armies. He imposed higher taxes on the wealthy nobility, which brought more revenue into the treasury. In addition, the king increased the amount of land owned by the monarchy.

Henry VII's reign was appreciated by the common people of England because he brought stability to the kingdom and ended civil war. In 1509, the king died and passed on a legacy of peace and prosperity to his son. At the age of seventeen, Henry VIII became king.

Chapter 3

The Young King

The coronation of a new king was a time of great celebration in England. In June 1509, Henry proceeded to the cathedral at Westminster, where he would be formally crowned. Along the way, crowds of people jostled each other to get a look at the seventeen-year-old monarch. Henry was a big man, much taller than most of his subjects, and he had a handsome face. "His majesty is the handsomest potentate [ruler] I ever set eyes on," one foreign observer said.[1] The new king wore a magnificent scarlet robe trimmed in fur. His clothes sparkled with diamonds, emeralds, and pearls.

Accompanying the king as he traveled along streets hung with tapestries was his new bride, Catherine of Aragon. They had been married a few weeks earlier after receiving special permission from the pope in Rome. Catholic law usually forbade a man to marry his brother's widow. During the Middle Ages, this type of marriage was considered incest, like marrying a member of the immediate family. But as Henry's father, the old king, lay dying, he had supposedly asked his son for a pledge to marry Catherine. Henry had agreed. Wearing a dress of white satin, Catherine entered Westminster along with her husband for the coronation.

It was a festive occasion because Henry was a very popular king. He was young, handsome, and seemed to have a natural ability to relate to his people. At one point during the coronation ceremony, when the spectators were asked if they wanted Henry for their monarch, great shouts of "Yea, yea" were heard.[2]

After the coronation, there was a celebration in the courtyard of Westminster. Workmen had created a miniature castle, and from its waterspouts flowed red and white wine. The festivities also included a tournament. Members of the nobility, dressed in shimmering armor and plumed helmets, mounted their horses and jousted against each other with long lances, as the king and queen watched from their royal box.

Soldier and Scholar

Although he did not take part in the tournament, Henry had a reputation as one of the most skilled warriors in England. He practiced daily with a huge double-sided sword and was such a good archer that he once defeated a group of his own bowmen in an archery contest. During the early years of his reign, Henry staged numerous jousting tournaments and frequently won them. He also enjoyed hunting animals. The young king would ride out into the fields with a group of companions at dawn and remain all day in the saddle. During the sixteenth century, hunting was an effective way of preparing for the cavalry battles of war. And the new king longed to distinguish himself on the battlefield. He had grown up listening to the stories of his famous ancestor, Henry V, who had won the great victory against the French at Agincourt. Henry VIII wanted to repeat this triumph.

However, there was another side to Henry, too. Unlike the majority of his subjects, the king was well-read and fluent in several languages. He was a poet who set his own poetry to music. He was also an accomplished musician. Indeed, his collection of musical instruments included more than twenty lutes.

Henry also corresponded with some of the leading scholars of Europe, including Desiderius Erasmus. Born in 1466, Erasmus of Rotterdam was a noted Dutch theologian (religious scholar). A devout Catholic, Erasmus nevertheless realized that the Church needed to be reformed. Men with enough money could buy themselves positions as cardinals or archbishops. Some of the popes in Rome had lived scandalously, keeping mistresses and having children. Henry met Erasmus several times when the theologian journeyed to England. Henry invited him to live there permanently. "It has been and is my earnest wish to

Source Document

Those who are closest to these [the theologians] in happiness are generally called "the religious" or "monks," both of which are deceiving names, since for the most part they stay as far away from religion as possible, and frequent every sort of place. I cannot, however, see how any life could be

more gloomy than the life of these monks if [Folly] did not assist them in many ways. Though most people detest these men so much that accidentally meeting one is considered to be bad luck, the monks themselves believe that they are magnificent creatures.[3]

Erasmus was one of the first thinkers to point out the need for reform in the Church.

restore Christ's religion to its primitive purity," Henry told Erasmus, adding that, together, they would "build again the Gospel of Christ."[4]

The King's Crusade

During the early part of his reign, Henry focused his attention on foreign affairs. The king wanted to make a great name for himself on the European stage, just as Henry V had done a century earlier. He also hoped to strengthen the Catholic religious faith in Europe. In 1513, England joined the Holy League, which included Pope Julius II as well as Holy Roman Emperor Maximilian of Germany.

Since the pope was the spiritual head of Christian Europe, which was then completely made up of Catholics, he had enormous power. Popes could excommunicate Catholics, or drive them out of the Church. This meant that, if they died while excommunicated, they could not reach eternal salvation in heaven. Most Catholics revered the pope as their religious leader and tried to follow the teachings of the Catholic Church so they could reach heaven. As Holy Roman emperor, Maximilian also possessed considerable power. Just as the pope claimed to be the spiritual head of the Catholic Church, the emperor claimed to be the Church's military defender on Earth. The emperor's position was confirmed by the pope, so they regarded themselves as natural allies. Since the tenth century, Holy Roman emperors had considered themselves the most powerful monarchs in Europe.

Maximilian controlled vast lands in Germany, Austria, and Italy.

The Holy League, led by the pope and Emperor Maximilian, declared war against France. Not only were the French the traditional enemies of England, but they were also trying to replace Pope Julius with someone else. French King Louis XII believed that Pope Julius and the Holy Roman emperor were far too powerful.

Henry VIII sailed for France with a mighty fleet of ships, one of them named after Erasmus. The fleet landed in Calais, a port controlled by England on the north coast of France. With approximately sixteen thousand troops, Henry headed south and besieged the French city of Therouanne. In one of the earliest uses of artillery, English troops dragged enormous guns in front of the city walls. Then the guns began pounding Therouanne into submission.

During the siege, French cavalry approached the city, hoping to drive off the English. Seeing themselves greatly outnumbered, the French retreated but the English pursued them. Henry joined the pursuit, which was called the Battle of the Spurs. The English captured the enemy's battle flags as well as many French knights, holding them for ransom. Eventually, Therouanne fell to the English Army, which also captured several other towns.

Following the successful campaign, Henry and his army returned home. The king had proven himself to be a tireless military campaigner. He had also captured the imagination of the English people, who began calling him Great Harry. Unfortunately, the war had accomplished very little. The power of France was not weakened. Meanwhile, the king had drained his treasury of most of the money that Henry VII had collected during his reign.

Henry and Wolsey

Although Henry hoped to achieve more glory on the battlefield, some of his most powerful advisors believed that England would be better off pursuing a policy of peace. Among them was Thomas Wolsey, England's chancellor—the king's chief minister and advisor. Born about 1473, Wolsey had become a priest and later the royal chaplain, or spiritual advisor, to Henry VII. Under the young Henry VIII, Wolsey took on greater responsibilities as counselor to the king.

A tireless worker, Wolsey routinely rose at 4:00 A.M. and stayed at his desk until evening. Henry leaned heavily on Wolsey's mastery of details and his experience in the affairs of state. Some observers believed that Wolsey, not Henry, made the major decisions of the realm, especially early in Henry's reign. However, the two men probably worked together on most important issues. Henry and his chancellor seemed to enjoy each other's company, dining together regularly. Nevertheless, many of the nobles in England resented Wolsey. He had not been born a member of the nobility. He was a commoner. However, he had been given more power than any noble in the realm. Like the

Chancellor Thomas Wolsey was one of Henry VIII's first and most influential advisors.

king, Wolsey enjoyed splendid clothes, and he had acquired great wealth.

In 1518, Wolsey brought together the major powers of Europe, including England and France, for a peace treaty. Its purpose was to prevent wars in the future. Two years later, he arranged a meeting between Henry and the new king of France, Francis I. The meeting occurred in Flanders—a part of France—on the Field of the Cloth of Gold. The field received this name because of the splendor that surrounded the event. On one side of the field, Francis had a large tent of gold brocade set up for himself. On the other side, Henry stayed in a palace that had been especially constructed for the occasion. The two kings then rode to the center of the field and met in a small pavilion. For the next three weeks, both kings and their followers engaged in feasting and tournaments. One of the highlights of the festivities was a wrestling match between Henry and Francis, in which the French king threw his rival to the ground.

Although both monarchs tried to remain friendly during the celebrations, very little actually changed between their two countries. There was enormous mistrust between the French and English. After all, England and France had been at war for around a hundred years during the fourteenth and fifteenth centuries.

A short time later, war broke out between France and Charles V. Charles was not only king of Spain, but he had also become Holy Roman emperor and controlled vast lands in central Europe. Henry decided to support Charles, who was the nephew of Catherine of Aragon, Henry's wife. However, the war in Europe would be overshadowed by an event of much greater significance—the Protestant Reformation, which would directly involve Henry VIII.

Chapter 4

The Reformation Begins

For more than a thousand years, Christians in Europe had all been part of the same Church, the Roman Catholic Church. The headquarters of the Church was in Rome. *Catholic* means universal, including everyone. The head of the Church was the bishop of Rome, also called the pope, the Italian word meaning father. The pope was considered the father of all Christians, their spiritual leader.

Since the pope was the head of Christianity, he had great power. Christians believed that they could only reach heaven by following the teachings of the Church. Many of these teachings were contained in the sacraments—religious rites that were believed to bestow grace on the people who participated in them. Sacraments removed sin and made people holy. If they died in this state of holiness, they could reach heaven.

One of these sacraments, for example, was confession. Good Christians were expected to confess their sins, or wrongdoings, to a member of the clergy, known as a priest. Another sacrament was communion. Christians believed that the body and blood of Jesus Christ were present in the bread and wine they received each Sunday at mass.

The Church and the Need for Reform

The Catholic Church was not only a spiritual institution. It controlled vast lands in Rome. Its bishops in other European countries also had large land holdings. The peasants who worked these lands paid taxes to the Church to support the clergy. In addition, the pope collected taxes from the monarchs of Europe. They sent the money to Rome, where some of it was used to erect magnificent churches. Unfortunately, some of the taxes also went toward maintaining the popes in an expensive lifestyle. They dressed in beautiful robes and gave lavish parties for their friends. The popes also spent church money to maintain armies to defend their lands, and these soldiers had to be paid to do their jobs.

Over the past few centuries, the Church constantly seemed to be running short of money. As a result, wealthy nobles were allowed to pay the pope to buy high positions in the Church. For example, a man with no religious training could buy himself a position as a bishop and take over all the lands that went with this title. He could hold many bishoprics if he had enough money to buy them. Some nobles bought positions for their sons. A child of five, for instance, might become a bishop or archbishop. These abuses began to trouble many truly spiritual people who believed the Church was losing its way. Not only were the bishops corrupt, but the pope himself seemed to be for sale to the highest bidder. Periodically, reform movements would arise in the Church to try to reduce the abuses. But these movements were usually followed by popes who allowed the abuses to increase again.

Popes were elected by a group of cardinals—the highest officials of the Church after the pope. During the twelfth and thirteenth centuries, however, the selection of the pope was often influenced by powerful noble families in Italy. The French kings resented the power of Italians to select a pope. In the fourteenth century, they decided to set up a rival pope in Avignon, France. For almost seventy years, there were two popes—one in Rome and the other in Avignon. This greatly weakened the authority of either pope. Many Christians became highly skeptical of the power and authority of Church leaders. Finally, a single pope was restored in Rome.

However, the lavish lifestyle of the popes and the abuses in the Church continued. Religious thinkers such as Erasmus called on the Church to reform itself, but it did nothing. Meanwhile, many political leaders in France and Germany were growing tired of being taxed by Rome to support the giant bureaucracy that had grown up in the Catholic Church. They had also begun to doubt whether the pope was the right person to be the moral leader of the Christian Church in Europe. During the fifteenth and sixteenth centuries, popes had indulged in luxuries and carried on affairs with women, even though Catholic priests were supposed to remain celibate. Popes readily took bribes and gave high positions in the Church to their relatives and friends. Some of these religious leaders were completely unqualified for their high positions, especially in Germany.

Martin Luther

During the early sixteenth century, the demand for reform grew loudest in Germany. One of the primary reformers was Martin Luther.

Born in 1483 in Saxony, a part of Germany, Martin Luther went to the University of Erfurt. Although he first intended to study law, Luther changed his mind and entered a monastery, where he became a monk. He studied the Bible carefully, and over time, he began to believe that its teachings differed significantly from the principles that were being practiced by the Roman Catholic Church. Luther was especially influenced by a passage from the biblical book of St. Paul in the New Testament, which said, "the just shall live by faith." For centuries, the Catholic Church had taught that individuals would be saved by performing good works, such as attending mass, giving money to the poor, or receiving the sacraments. Luther decided, based on the passage in St. Paul, that good works would not lead to salvation. Only faith in God could assure an individual's place in heaven.

Luther's beliefs were put to the test in 1517, when a Dominican friar named Johann Tetzel came to Saxony to sell indulgences. Tetzel preached that anyone who purchased an "indulgence" would be forgiven for his or her sins. Money from the indulgences was used by the Catholic Church to build a huge cathedral, St. Peter's, in Rome. Martin Luther believed that the entire concept of indulgences was ridiculous. He said that, if the Church had the power to forgive those who paid for indulgences, it should also have the power to forgive everyone, even if they did not pay.

Luther wrote down his opinions of church practices in the form of ninety-five theses, or statements, and posted them on the door of the castle church in Wittenberg, Germany, on October 31, 1517. Although some historians doubt Luther actually posted his theses, believing he simply gave out his work to influential thinkers, this form of protest was a common way at the time

Martin Luther started the Protestant Reformation in Europe when he put out his famous Ninety-five Theses.

Source Document

It was in the year 1517, when the profligate monk Tetzel, a worthy servant of the pope and the devil—for I am certain that the pope is the agent of the devil on earth—came among us selling indulgences, maintaining their efficacy, and impudently practising on the credulity of the people. When I beheld this unholy and detestable traffic taking place in open day, and thereby sanctioning the most villainous crimes, I could not, though I was then but a young doctor of divinity, refrain from protesting against it in the strongest manner, not only as directly contrary to the Scriptures, but as opposed to the canons of the church itself.[1]

Martin Luther gave this account of what led him to start the Protestant Reformation in Germany.

for scholars to express their opinions on important issues.

At first, Luther called on the pope to clean up the abuses in the Church, but the pope ignored him. In 1520, Luther wrote his *Address to the Christian Nobility of the German Nation*, urging noblemen to lead reforms in the Church. At this time, Germany was not a united country. It was an area of many small states, each with its own ruler. Although all of them were Catholics, many were eager to end the Church's authority over them.

Common people also flocked to Martin Luther's call for reform. They had grown tired of abuses in the Church and they were skeptical of local priests who did not always set a good example. Some priests even committed the very sins they warned others to avoid. In his writings, Luther attacked the use of sacraments, such as confession, in which priests gave people forgiveness for their sins. Luther emphasized that every person could be saved by faith alone and did not need a priest to serve as a "middle man." For his position on these issues, Luther was excommunicated from the Church.

Defender of the Faith

Luther's writings spread quickly to many parts of Europe. The invention of the printing press in the fifteenth century meant that books and pamphlets could be printed more rapidly, allowing more people to read them. Without the printing press, it is unlikely that the writings of Luther would have been read by so many people and had such a wide impact.

In 1521, after Luther's works had found their way to England, they were burned in a public ceremony. The burning was attended by Thomas Wolsey, who had become a cardinal of the Catholic Church. But Wolsey was not the only one opposed to Protestantism, as the new religious movement aimed at breaking away from the Catholic Church was called. That same year, King Henry VIII published a book called *The Defense of the Seven Sacraments*. Although the king probably did not write the entire book himself, he worked with the learned scholars of his court who put it together. It was not a scholarly work. Instead, it was written in a style that most people who could read would understand. Because it was written by a king, the book became a powerful response to Martin Luther's statements.

In the book, Henry defended the sacraments— many of which Luther questioned—as a vital part of religious belief, and reiterated the fact that the pope was the religious leader of the Catholic Church. A copy of the book was presented to Pope Leo X, who read it enthusiastically. Shortly afterward, the pope gave Henry a new title: Defender of the Faith. Pope Leo expected Henry to defend the Catholic Church against Protestantism. Henry was supposed to lead the effort to get Protestantism out of England and the rest of Europe.

Among the ideas presented in Henry's book was his strong defense of the Catholic Church's position on marriage. The Church emphasized that, once a couple had married, they could never divorce. Henry's words would shortly prove to be an enormous embarrassment to him as he entered the most critical stage of his reign—the controversy surrounding his divorce from Queen Catherine of Aragon.

Chapter 5

Henry's Marriage Crisis

When she became queen of England in 1509, Catherine of Aragon was one of the most learned women in the English realm. She had been raised by her mother, Isabella of Spain, to be the intellectual equal of a man. Catherine knew how to speak several languages fluently, read widely, and had a broad knowledge of the law.

As wife to the king, Catherine gave Henry her complete loyalty. She rejoiced as much in his triumphs on the battlefield or in politics as the king himself did. Henry VIII also appreciated the common sense advice she gave him in matters of state. Unfortunately, Catherine could not give the king something that he wanted very much—a son, an heir to his kingdom.

Early in their marriage, Catherine had given birth to a son, but he had lived only two months. There were

Queen Catherine of Aragon was one of the best educated women of her time.

two more boys, one born in 1513 and another in 1514, but both were still-born (dead at birth).

In 1516, the queen gave birth to a girl, named Mary, who grew into a healthy child. Both Henry and Catherine doted on this little girl. But the king was hesitant to make a girl his heir. According to English law, when a woman married, her husband took control of her land and titles. Therefore, whoever married Mary would rule as king in England. That meant the next monarch would not be a Tudor. Only once before in English history, during the twelfth century, had a woman, Matilda (sometimes called Maud), taken the throne as queen. The realm had been plunged into a bloody civil war. Henry did not want to see these events repeated. Nor did he want England to experience another period of turmoil like the War of the Roses, which had ended less than a half century earlier and might occur again.

Without a male heir, the Tudor dynasty seemed to be in jeopardy. The English people became especially worried during the 1520s, when they heard that Henry had narrowly escaped serious injury during a jousting tournament. A fragment from the lance of his opponent entered the king's helmet and might have killed him. Luckily, he was unharmed. Shortly afterward, the king experienced a serious fall while hunting. The accident might have killed someone less robust. These incidents were a constant reminder that there was no male heir to sit on the throne if anything happened to the king.

Henry tried to deal with this problem in 1525. Several years earlier, he had sired a son, but by a woman who was not his wife. Kings often took mistresses, and Henry was no different. Bessie Blount, who was considered the most beautiful woman at court, had given Henry a son in 1519. The boy was named Henry Fitzroy. When he was only six years old, the king made the boy a duke. The king also gave his illegitimate son other titles that made him the most important noble in England. Some of the king's subjects believed that Henry would name the boy his heir. But since illegitimate sons usually were not accepted as kings, the English people might not have supported Fitzroy.

Henry and Anne

About 1526, an event occurred that would have a much greater impact on England and the future of the Tudors. King Henry VIII fell in love with a young woman named Anne Boleyn. Nicknamed Nan, she had been born around 1501. By that time, the Boleyn family had been involved in politics for several decades. One of Anne's great-grandfathers had served as Lord Mayor of London in 1457 and had purchased a castle for his family in Kent, south of the capital. Anne's father, Thomas Boleyn, had married Lady Elizabeth Howard. She was the eldest daughter of the Duke of Norfolk, one of England's most powerful nobles.

Thomas Boleyn, who spoke several languages fluently, served Henry VIII as ambassador to France. He had helped arrange the meeting between Henry VIII and Francis I on the Field of the Cloth of Gold. While Boleyn was ambassador, his daughter Anne became an attendant to the French queen.

Anne remained in France for six or seven years and returned to England around 1521. She then became an attendant to Queen Catherine. Anne was about twenty years old. She had dark hair, dark eyes, and olive skin. Although she was not considered the most beautiful woman, she was known for her sharp wit, and unlike most women of the period, she spoke French and other languages. Anne had already caught the attention of several men. One of them, Henry Percy, whose father was the powerful Earl of Northumberland, may have even proposed marriage. But Percy's father had opposed the match, and it ended.

Shortly afterward, Anne caught the attention of someone far more powerful—the king. Henry began writing love letters to her, some of them in French, which was then the language of courtly love. From time to time, Anne was away from court and the king missed her. "Consider well," Henry wrote, "how greatly my absence from you grieves me; I hope it is not your will that it should be so. . . ." The king also pledged his lasting affection to Anne and promised to serve "only you."[1] He wanted Anne to become his mistress, but she refused. Gradually, the king decided on a much bolder plan.

A New Queen

For some time, the king had been trying to decide how to deal with the problem of having no legitimate male heir. The king still admired Catherine, who had been his wife for almost twenty years. They dined together regularly and presided over many royal events at court. Many of the English people revered the queen, who was widely known for her piety. But the queen was now too old to have any more children. She could never give Henry the son he wanted.

The king had become convinced that his marriage to Catherine might have been cursed from the beginning. Henry, who read the Bible regularly, was very familiar with a line from Leviticus in the Old Testament. It said: "If a man shall take his brother's wife . . . they shall be childless." Henry believed that the line really meant that the couple would have no sons, not no children at all. The king decided that the

Source Document

Myne awne Sweetheart, this shall be to advertise you of the great ellingness [loneliness] that I find here since your departing, for I ensure you, me thinketh the Tyme longer since your departing now last than I was wont to do a whole Fortnight; I think your Kindness and my Fervence of Love causeth it, for otherwise I wolde not thought it possible, that for so little a while it should have grieved me, but now that I am comeing toward you, me thinketh my Pains by half released. . . . I have spent above IIII Hours this Day, which caused me now to write the shorter Letter to you at this Tyme, because some Payne in my Head, wishing my self (specially an Evening) in my Sweethearts Armes. . . .[2]

Henry VIII wrote this love letter to Anne Boleyn in 1533.

only way for him to have a son was to marry someone else. In 1527, he asked his wife for a divorce. Henry wanted to make Anne Boleyn his new queen.

Divorce was strictly forbidden by the Catholic Church. Nevertheless, the Church did make occasional exceptions, especially for the powerful. The king's sister Mary, for example, had married the powerful Duke of Suffolk, who had already been divorced twice. Queen Margaret of Scotland, another sister of the king, had divorced her husband to marry someone else in 1527. Henry, therefore, believed that he might also be permitted to marry again. In addition, the king was not really asking for a divorce as his sister had done. Although it is often called a divorce, Henry was actually requesting an annulment, which would state that his marriage to Catherine had never been legal. He believed that his first marriage was invalid because the pope should never have granted him permission to marry Catherine in 1509. According to the Bible, by marrying his brother's widow, he would not be able to fulfill one of his primary duties as king—to produce a son and heir.

By having his marriage declared invalid and marrying Anne, the king would finally be able to fulfill his responsibilities to England. As one historian put it: "The dictates of the King's conscience and the dictates of the King's desire thus happily joined. Both told him to get rid of Queen Catherine."[3]

The King's "Great Matter"

As the pope's representative in England and the most powerful political counselor to the king, Cardinal Thomas Wolsey was given the task of resolving Henry's marriage problem. In 1527, Wolsey began an official examination of the marriage. Although he listened carefully to the king's views, the cardinal also realized that the Bible did not say "no sons" but "childless." Henry and Catherine had a daughter, Mary, so their marriage had not necessarily been cursed. In addition, there was another Bible passage in the book of Deuteronomy that stated it was "the duty of a husband's brother" to his childless widow to "go in unto her, and take her to him to wife." Henry had done exactly as this passage had directed. Therefore, the Bible contained two passages that were in conflict with each other. One supported the marriage to Catherine, the other seemed to oppose it.

Was an earlier pope, Julius II, correct when he permitted the marriage? Or should his decision now be overturned by the current pope, Clement VII? Queen Catherine wanted the Pope Clement to decide in her favor and forbid the divorce. She was convinced that her marriage was not invalid and that she had not been living in sin with Henry. She was also certain that their daughter, Mary, was legitimate. In addition, Catherine had no intention of being cast aside by the king and the woman he loved, Anne Boleyn.

Many of the English people supported Catherine. They saw a devout, middle-aged queen being replaced

53

by a younger woman. The English cheered Catherine when she appeared in public, even though they knew she could not produce sons. They jeered Anne.

The Queen and the Emperor

Queen Catherine not only had the support of the English people, but she also had another powerful ally—her nephew Charles V. As king of Spain and Holy Roman emperor, Charles was the leading monarch in Europe. In 1526, he had defeated Francis I of France, the major power opposed to him. The French gave up the territories they held in Italy, leaving Charles in control. Pope Clement VII, however, believed Charles was too powerful and threatened the independence of the pope in Rome. French King Francis I made an alliance with the pope, and their armies went to war against Charles. In 1527, the Holy Roman emperor's soldiers marched into Rome and began looting the city. Clement VII suddenly found himself under the control of Charles V.

This situation had a direct impact on the marital affairs of England's king. Pope Clement was caught between two powerful monarchs. On the one hand, there was King Henry, whom the pope had called "Defender of the Faith." Henry had sent ambassadors to Rome to plead his case that his marriage should be declared invalid. The ambassadors also carried a letter from Cardinal Wolsey telling the pope that Anne Boleyn was a highly virtuous woman and worthy to be a queen. But the pope also had to deal with Charles V, who controlled the fate of Rome. Charles did not want to see his aunt cast aside for Anne and lose her position as queen of England. Pope Clement delayed and tried to put off making any decision.

Meanwhile, Henry had convinced himself that the pope would eventually decide in his favor and allow him to marry Anne. As he wrote to her in 1528: "Darling, you and I shall have our desired end, which should be more to my heart's ease, and more quietness to my mind, than any other thing in the world."[4] When Anne appeared at court, she spent more and more time with Henry, hunting with the king and presiding over celebrations with him. He was clearly indicating to everyone that Anne was to be his next queen. But Pope Clement still refused to make a decision.

Finally, in 1528, the pope sent an ambassador, Cardinal Lorenzo Campeggio, to England. Campeggio and Cardinal Wolsey were expected to preside over a special court that would rule on whether the king's marriage to Catherine should be declared invalid. It took several months for Campeggio to make the trip across Europe to London. He was an elderly man in poor health, but he was considered an expert on church law. After his arrival in England, Campeggio and Cardinal Wolsey went to visit Queen Catherine. Both men pleaded with her to give up the marriage to the king and enter a nunnery. She could declare that the marriage never should have occurred, that she was not really Henry's wife, and become a nun. But Catherine refused. She said she was the "true and legitimate wife of the King, her husband."[5] Since the queen was unwilling to give up her marriage, the two cardinals called a court of nobles and clergy into session.

Henry hoped for a favorable verdict from the court. Cardinal Wolsey also realized that his future as chief counselor to the king depended on his ability to have the marriage dissolved. Although Wolsey had served the king faithfully for many years, he had made powerful enemies. Some of England's aristocrats were jealous of the honors that the king had given to Wolsey. In addition, they disliked the cardinal's arrogant personality. Among those who opposed Wolsey were Thomas Boleyn and his friends, who had become a powerful group in England because of Anne Boleyn's relationship with the king. Anne and Henry were willing to let Wolsey convene the court and try to win a favorable verdict. But if he failed, he might lose his position in England. What neither Wolsey nor the king realized was that Campeggio had been given strict instructions by the pope. As one historian said: "Campeggio knew he was under papal orders to avoid a decision at all costs."[6] This way, the pope would not have to anger King Henry or Charles V.

On June 21, 1529, King Henry VIII and Queen Catherine appeared before the court. The king reaffirmed his position that the marriage was invalid. Then the queen spoke. She left her seat and kneeled before the king. "I beseech you," she began, "for all the love that hath been between us, let me have justice and right, take of me some pity and compassion. . . . I take God and all the world to witness that I have been to you a true, humble and obedient wife, ever comfortable to your will and pleasure. . . ."[7] After she finished speaking, the queen turned and left the court. The court crier summoned her back because the king did not want her to leave. He wanted her to agree to a divorce. She refused. She never returned to the court again.

Campeggio heard the rest of the evidence, then adjourned to consider his decision. But, as the pope had instructed him, the old cardinal never intended to give a verdict.

By this time, King Henry and Anne Boleyn both realized that Cardinal Wolsey could do nothing to help them. The king took all of Wolsey's power away from him. The cardinal was later accused of treason for having secret dealings with the French. But he died in 1530 before ever standing trial.

King Henry now decided to use a different approach to settle his marriage crisis—an approach that would transform the Church in England.

Chapter 6

Henry Launches a Reformation

In 1530, King Henry seemed no closer to his goals of marrying Anne Boleyn and siring a male heir. To gather support for his divorce from Catherine, the king sent his agents to the European continent. They were ordered to confer with scholars and to search the libraries of great universities—all in an effort to find evidence that would allow Henry to marry again. This was part of the king's campaign to win the public relations battle for his marriage to Anne. The king's agents did succeed in convincing eight universities, including the prestigious Sorbonne in Paris, to support the king. But it was not enough to convince the pope. Clement VII had recalled Campeggio to Rome and had decided that Henry's case must be decided there instead of in England. This would give the pope complete control over the decision.

Meanwhile, in 1529, the king had called a meeting of his Parliament, which would hold sessions for the next seven years. Parliament was made up of two houses. The lower house, or Commons, included representatives from England's towns and cities. In the upper house, the Lords, sat the great aristocrats of the realm as well as the bishops of the Catholic Church. Parliament did not meet all the time. The king usually called it for special occasions—such as granting new taxes or approving a great change in England's political situation.

Such a change had occurred with the fall of Cardinal Wolsey, who had been Henry's chief minister for many years. Many people resented Wolsey because of his enormous wealth. Members of the clergy were expected to be religious men, not interested in worldly possessions. Wolsey had seemed to symbolize the abuses practiced by some of the Catholic clergy. In 1529, Henry discussed these abuses with the ambassador to England from the Holy Roman Empire. The king told the ambassador that the pope and his cardinals were much too worldly. Henry added that Martin Luther had been right in criticizing the abuses of the Catholic Church. The king said that the Church needed reform. He added that, as sovereign of the realm and one of the political leaders of Europe, perhaps he should lead the reforming effort. However, he never intended to adopt the new religion started by Luther or anybody else.

Reform Begins

As it turned out, the king and his Parliament would start a reform movement together. It would be called the Reformation Parliament. Shortly after Parliament began to meet in 1529, the House of Commons submitted a petition to the king describing some of the abuses of the clergy. Members of Parliament demanded to know why the clergy should be allowed to own worldly goods, as Wolsey had done. The petition also asked why bishops should have more than one parish. Some of them were in charge of several large churches. They grew rich off the donations of parishioners and the lands these churches owned. One historian explained: "The Church excited hatred by the wealth it had and the wealth it sought. About one-third of England's lands were in ecclesiastical hands. . . ."[1] Some of the bishops lived so far away from their churches that they could not minister to the needs of their congregations. The Commons wanted this practice to be stopped.

In the House of Lords, where the bishops sat, there was enormous opposition to the petition from the Commons. The king, however, supported the members of the lower house. Henry pressured the bishops to agree to some changes in Church practices. No longer would members of the clergy be allowed to live apart from their congregations or lead more than one church. Anyone guilty of these offenses would be brought before an English court. In the past, the pope had had jurisdiction over these offenses. He would no

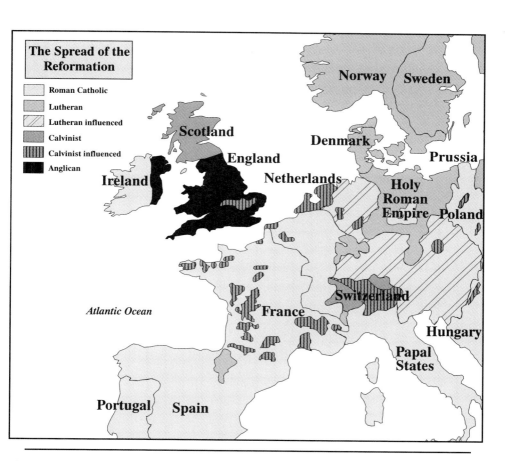

The Spread of the
Reformation

- Roman Catholic
- Lutheran
- Lutheran influenced
- Calvinist
- Calvinist influenced
- Anglican

Norway Sweden

Scotland

Denmark

Prussia

England

Ireland

Netherlands

Holy
Roman
Empire Poland

Atlantic Ocean

Switzerland

France

Hungary

Papal
States

Portugal Spain

*The different nations of Europe were torn in their loyalties to
Protestantism and Catholicism during the Reformation.*

longer be given this power, and any clergyman who appealed to Rome to overturn a state ruling would be fined.

This new law limited the power of the pope. Henry hoped to use the law to put pressure on Clement VII to make a favorable decision on the king's divorce. But the law seemed to have no effect, because the pope still refused to make any decision. So Henry decided to increase the pressure. In England, as in other countries, the Catholic Church maintained its own courts. Here, the clergy could be tried for offenses, such as sexual abuses, theft, and arson. In 1530, Henry charged the clergy with using the power of the Church courts to undermine the authority of the royal courts. The clergy, who felt threatened, agreed to pay a huge fine to the king to retain the clerical courts.

But this was not enough to satisfy Henry. He insisted that the English Catholic leaders recognize him as the supreme head of the English Church. This was a direct challenge to the power of the pope, and many of the English bishops refused to grant Henry this authority. "We cannot grant this unto the king," explained John Fisher, the elderly bishop of Rochester, without ending "our unity with the see of Rome [Roman Catholic Church] . . . we renounce the unity of the Christian world . . . to be drowned in the waves of all heresies . . . and divisions."[2]

To question the authority of the pope and the Church seemed, to many clergymen, to question the authority of God. The Catholic Church was considered one of the strongest institutions in Europe. Its religious teachings provided structure for the lives of millions of people. Without this structure, the entire fabric of Christianity might be torn apart, causing chaos and upheaval. Henry VIII seemed to be challenging this unity, just as Martin Luther was doing in Germany. In addition, the king was putting his political power over the religious power of the pope.

The religious leaders of the English Catholic Church strongly opposed Henry. Led by John Fisher, the bishops would only agree to be guided by the king's authority "as far as the law of God allows."[3] In other words, God's law, as symbolized by the pope, was still considered higher than the king's.

Henry's Changing Position

The king's insistence on becoming the supreme head of the English Church was, in part, another attempt to put pressure on Pope Clement VII. Henry hoped that, by threatening to limit the

John Fisher (right) was one of the main opponents of Henry VIII's religious reforms.

power of the pope, he might persuade Clement to give in to the king's demands for a divorce. But if this did not work, the king might also have been preparing to take over control of the Church in England so he could obtain a divorce without the permission of the pope.

About this time, the king read *Obedience of the Christian Man*, written by the Protestant theologian William Tyndale. The book had probably been given to Henry by Anne Boleyn, who sympathized with Martin Luther's Protestant teachings. Tyndale argued that a king should expect the complete allegiance of his subjects. He should not share it with the pope in Rome. "This is the book for me and all kings to read," Henry said.[4] In Germany, Luther believed that rulers should be supreme in their own realms. Many princes there embraced Protestantism and no longer recognized the power of Rome. Thus Henry's effort to become head of the Church in England was an attempt to strengthen and consolidate the power of the king.

The Rise of Thomas Cromwell

During the early 1530s, the king began to pressure Parliament to pass a series of reforms that would transform the Church in England. Leading this effort was one of the king's counselors, Thomas Cromwell. Born in 1485, the year Henry VII had become king, Cromwell was the son of a blacksmith. As a young man, he had decided to leave England and seek his fortune as a soldier in Italy. Later, he went to work for

Thomas Cromwell was Henry VIII's chief advisor during the start of the English Reformation.

a banker in Florence, Itlay, then traveled to the Netherlands. For many years, there had been brisk trade between England and the Netherlands. English wool and unfinished cloth were sent to the Netherlands. There, they were turned into finished fabrics by Dutch artisans. Cromwell worked for a trading company where he became an expert in financial matters.

Eventually, Thomas Cromwell returned to London and trained to become a lawyer. By 1524, he had gone to work for the king's advisor Cardinal Wolsey. Here, Cromwell gained a great deal of experience in the important government affairs of England. Like Wolsey, Cromwell believed in working long hours, but in other ways, he was quite different from the great cardinal. Cromwell did not have a lavish lifestyle, and he resented the worldliness of the clergy. His religious beliefs were much closer to Martin Luther's than to the pope's. And, like King Henry VIII, Cromwell believed that the power of the Roman Catholic Church should be reduced in England.

After Wolsey's fall in 1529, Cromwell remained in government service. He served in Parliament, where he helped shape the petition that came before the king to limit the privileges of the clergy. Then he became a counselor to King Henry VIII and helped direct the legislation to reform the Church through Parliament. In 1532, for example, Cromwell drafted a new bill that was designed to accomplish several things. First, any new laws that were passed by clergymen to govern themselves would have to be approved by the king. Second, a royal committee would be appointed to look at any past clerical legislation to determine which of those laws should remain in force.

The Archbishop of Canterbury was the most powerful Church leader in England. As archbishop, William Warham refused to agree to legislation that would make the clergy subordinate to the king. Henry was upset by this and summoned a group of representatives from Parliament. He produced a copy of the oath to obey the pope that all bishops swore. "Well-beloved subjects," the king began, "we thought that the clergy of our realm had been our [Henry's] subjects wholly, but now we have well perceived that they be but half our subjects, yea, and scarce our subjects."[5] Warham and some of the other bishops refused to agree to the new legislation. Nevertheless, Henry and Thomas Cromwell succeeded in winning approval of the Submission of the Clergy Act from church leaders in England during 1532. According to this legislation, no new laws designed to govern the clergy could be passed without Henry's approval. Thus, the king was taking control of the English Church.

As a result of this new law, England's chancellor, Sir Thomas More, resigned his office. King Henry had appointed More to replace Cardinal Wolsey. More was a friend of Erasmus and an internationally famous scholar. He had also written a widely read book called *Utopia*. It discussed the elements of a perfect society on Earth. More was a friend of Queen Catherine. He did not agree with the king's attempt to get a divorce from his wife. Although More believed that the Catholic Church needed reform, he did not want to see the structure of the Church overthrown. More strongly believed that the pope should remain the head of the Church, and that England should continue to obey Rome in all spiritual matters.

The Crisis Deepens

However, King Henry and his powerful political associate, Thomas Cromwell, continued to push their reforms through Parliament. In 1532, they submitted a bill called the Act of Annates. The annates were fees that newly appointed English bishops were expected to pay to Rome when they took up their positions. This act cut off those payments. It also stated that new bishops could now be appointed by the king without the consent of Rome. Some members of Parliament believed the king was going too far in eliminating the traditional role of the pope. King Henry was forced to go to Parliament on three separate occasions to urge

Source Document

As he told us of many things that were amiss in those newdiscovered countries, so he reckoned up not a few things from which patterns might be taken for correcting the errors of these nations among whom we live; of which an account may be given, as I have already promised, at some other time; for at present I intend only to relate those particulars that he told us of the manners and laws of the Utopians. . . .[6]

Thomas More wrote Utopia, *an account of a fictitious country where the system of laws has created a paradise for the people who live there.*

the members to support him before they finally agreed to the new legislation.

Even at this point, however, Henry may have been trying only to apply as much pressure as possible on Pope Clement so he would agree to the divorce. The pope, however, had refused to grant the decision Henry wanted. Late in 1532, Henry realized he could no longer wait for the pope to act. Anne Boleyn had become pregnant. The king confidently believed that she would give birth to a son and give him a male heir. But to make sure that the heir was legitimate, Anne and Henry needed to be married. In January 1533, Anne and Henry were secretly married. To make sure that the marriage was approved, Henry took matters into his own hands.

In 1533, King Henry won approval from Parliament for the Act in Restraint of Appeals. According to this act, any decision made by an English court regarding religious issues or any other matters could not be appealed to Rome. "Of all the Reformation acts," wrote one historian on the period, "that in Restraint of Appeals, passed in February–March 1533, was at once the most epoch-making, the most clear in its statement of principles, the most central to the . . . Reformation."[7] The act stated that England was a kingdom with only one ruler who was subject to no other power on Earth. All his subjects must obey him in all matters, including spiritual ones. The act had been drafted by Thomas Cromwell and his assistants.

For his work, Cromwell was appointed the king's chief minister.

In 1532, William Warham died. The king chose a close ally, Thomas Cranmer, to be the new Archbishop of Canterbury. Under the Act of Annates, Cranmer would retain his position even if the pope did not approve of him. On May 23, 1533, Cranmer, now the most powerful bishop in England, declared that King Henry VIII's marriage to Catherine of Aragon had never existed. The Act in Restraint of Appeals meant that this decision could not be appealed to Church authorities in Rome. Therefore, the king became free to marry Anne Boleyn. Less than a week later, Anne formally became the queen of England.

Pope Clement reacted sharply, excommunicating King Henry VIII from the Church. This meant that, if the king died, he would be in a state of sin and would go to hell for all eternity, according to Christian beliefs. Because the king was no longer a member of the Roman Catholic Church, Rome gave its permission to any of his subjects to overthrow him and replace Henry with a devout Catholic king who would bring England back to the church in Rome. Of course, no revolt occurred. But some of the king's subjects were highly critical of the divorce and even called for his overthrow. Among them was a nun named Elizabeth Barton and her followers. They were arrested and executed.

Anne Boleyn (seen here) was at the center of King Henry VIII's controversial decision to divorce his first wife.

An Heir to the Throne

In September 1533, Queen Anne gave birth to the child who had been long awaited by her new husband. To Henry's disappointment, however, the baby was a girl. She was named Elizabeth. Despite her gender, the king decided that she should become his heir, at least until Anne gave birth to a boy. In 1534, Parliament passed the Succession Act, stating that the children of Henry and Anne should become heirs to the throne of England. The act also included a section charging anyone who criticized the marriage with treason. In addition, Cromwell inserted a clause that required every adult to swear an oath to support the Succession Act.

While most of the king's subjects seemed to be willing to swear the oath, many of them still believed that the king should never have divorced Catherine of Aragon. Despite their views, however, the old queen had been pushed aside and forced to live in a drafty castle with crumbling walls. She was also forbidden to see her daughter, Mary, who lived separately.

Catherine died of cancer in 1536. She had never fully accepted the divorce from Henry VIII.

Meanwhile, Parliament continued to reform the Church under the direction of the king. In 1534, Henry was declared head of the Church by the Act of Supremacy. It was now called the Church of England. By this time, the king had gone much too far for men like Bishop John Fisher and Sir Thomas More. Fisher refused to recognize Henry's new position. He had even written to Holy Roman Emperor Charles V, urging him to invade England and overthrow the king. This was treason, and Fisher was arrested and taken to prison in the Tower of London. A day later, More was also led away to the Tower for refusing to swear an oath to support the Succession Act. Soon afterward, the former chancellor was brought before Cromwell and Archbishop Cranmer and asked if he might change his mind. In More's eyes, however, the Succession Act meant that the pope no longer had any authority in England. The pope had forbidden Henry's marriage to Anne Boleyn. The English Church had broken with Rome. As More explained, "I cannot swear, without the jeoparding of my soul to perpetual damnation."[8]

For more than a year, More and Fisher remained in the Tower. Other opponents of Henry VIII's religious reforms were also imprisoned and some were then executed for not swearing to support the English Reformation or the king's new position as head of the Church. Finally, on June 22, 1535, John Fisher left the

Source Document

. . . be it enacted, by authority of this present Parliament, that the king, our sovereign lord, his heirs and successors, kings of this realm, shall be taken, accepted, and reputed the only supreme head in earth of the Church of England, called Anglicans Ecclesia; and shall have and enjoy, annexed and united to the imperial crown of this realm, as well the title and style thereof, as all honors, dignities, preeminences, jurisdictions, privileges, authorities, immunities, profits, and commodities to the said dignity of the supreme head of the same Church belonging and appertaining; and that our said sovereign lord, his heirs and successors, kings of this realm, shall have full power and authority from time to time to visit, repress, redress, record, order, correct, restrain, and amend all such errors, heresies, abuses, offenses, contempts and enormities, whatsoever they be. . . .[9]

The Act of Supremacy of 1534 legally made Henry VIII head of the Church in England.

Thomas More was executed for his opposition to Henry VIII's religious reforms.

Tower of London. Although he was almost too weak to walk, Fisher was taken to the scaffold and executed. A short time later, Thomas More also lost his life on the executioner's block. As he prepared to die, More declared: "I die loyal to God and the King. But to God first of all."[10]

The deaths of two distinguished men such as More and Fisher sent shock waves throughout England and Europe. Some of Henry's subjects who had supported the Reformation now began to wonder if the king had become a tyrant.

Chapter 7

Henry's Realm in Turmoil

In January 1536, King Henry was competing in a jousting tournament. As he charged his opponent in the center of the field, the king was suddenly toppled from his horse and knocked harshly to the ground. He lay unconscious for two hours while his courtiers gathered around him, hoping for his recovery. Henry apparently suffered no lasting harm. But when Queen Anne heard about the accident, she was reportedly so upset that it may have caused her to miscarry. The queen was only three months pregnant with her second child. If she had been able to complete her pregnancy, it is possible that Henry might have finally received the male heir he had wanted for so long.

When the king eventually reached Anne's side, he showed very little concern for the queen's health. He simply remarked, "I see that God will not give me male children." Then he added, "When you are up, I will come and speak to you."[1]

The king was already losing interest in Anne. He was growing frustrated with her inability to produce a son. His attentions were now focused on another woman, twenty-year-old Jane Seymour, one of the queen's attendants.

Jane Seymour

Jane was the daughter of Sir John Seymour, who had fought valiantly for the king's father, Henry VII. Seymour had accompanied Henry VIII during his meeting with King Francis at the Field of the Cloth of Gold. He later received an important position as one of the king's attendants at court. Jane was one of ten children, and the oldest of John Seymour's daughters. She was known at court for her beautiful complexion, sensible nature, and above all, her virtue and purity.[2]

King Henry had fallen in love with Jane and wanted to marry her. But no marriage could occur until the king had divorced his current queen, Anne Boleyn. Henry decided that he did not want what had happened with Queen Catherine to occur again. Catherine had had a spotless reputation and broad support among her subjects. Although Henry had eventually divorced her, she had fought against him for many years, embarrassing the king and costing him the loyalty of some of the English people.

This time, the king's chief minister, Thomas Cromwell, led a secret commission that was instructed to uncover some wrongdoing by Queen Anne. This would give the king a reason to remove her. Cromwell's commission found evidence that Anne had been involved in several affairs with other men (although most historians doubt the charges were valid). One of them was a lute player at court named Mark Smeaten. Another was Anne's own brother. All the men accused were rounded up and arrested. Only Smeaten, who may have been tortured, admitted to a relationship with Anne, although she denied everything. Still, it was enough to condemn her. Anne was found guilty of adultery and beheaded on May 19, 1536. By the end of the month, King Henry had married Jane Seymour.

Cromwell and the Protestant Reformation

As the king's chief minister, Thomas Cromwell served his monarch very effectively. He had helped Henry initiate the Protestant Reformation. Cromwell was involved in helping Henry remove one wife so he could marry another. In 1535, Cromwell had also been named vice-regent, with power to act for the king in all the religious affairs of England. Since Cromwell was a lawyer, not a priest, his appointment meant that the king and his advisors, not the bishops, were now in control of the English Church.

As part of his reformation in England, the king had decided to dissolve the monasteries. In Germany, Martin Luther had led a similar movement. These

Jane Seymour is often considered the favorite of Henry VIII's wives.

religious houses included abbeys and nunneries. Some of them controlled large land holdings that were worth vast sums of money. They also had expensive gold chalices and silver plates that were used in religious services.

Henry wanted control of this wealth for several reasons. The money would enable him to build armies and finance any wars he might have to fight against a European power, such as France, the pope, or the Holy Roman emperor, all of whom opposed him because he had broken with the Catholic Church. He could also reward his supporters with some of the land from the monasteries. As Henry was changing the religious beliefs of England, he needed the loyalty of the powerful nobles. Many of them were greedy for additional land, and they would give the king their support in exchange for new land holdings.

Henry reasoned that, if he dissolved the monasteries, there might not be too much opposition from the English people. They often regarded the monks as lazy men who lived immoral lives. According to one estimate, less than 5 percent of the income that the monasteries received from contributions or from selling the crops grown on their lands went to help the poor and needy.[3] The monasteries did not have broad support among the king's subjects.

In 1535, Cromwell sent out inspectors to the smaller monasteries to find out if there were any evidence of immorality among the monks or mismanagement of finances. The inspectors had been carefully instructed

Source Document

In my most humble manner I have me commended unto your good lordship, ascertaining the same that I have pulled down the image of Our Lady at Caversham, whereunto was great pilgrimage. The image is plated over with silver, and I have put it in a chest fast locked and nailed up, and by the next barge that cometh from Reading to London it shall be brought to your lordship. I have also pulled down the place she stood in, with all other ceremonies, as lights, shrowds, crosses, and images of wax hanging about the chapel, and have defaced the same thoroughly in eschewing of any further resort thither.[4]

Thomas Cromwell's agents sent him this report, telling him of their progress in forcing the end of Catholic practices in England.

that they must find abuses to support the king's desire to dissolve the monasteries. They uncovered evidence at many of the abbeys and priories. After Cromwell received the report of the inspectors, a bill was introduced in Parliament in 1536 to dissolve the smaller monasteries. When the abuses uncovered in these houses were read to the members of Parliament, they shouted, "Down with them."[5]

The dissolution of the smaller monasteries began immediately. Over the next four years, the larger houses would also be eliminated. Most of the work was done peacefully. The abbot or prior who ran a house was given a generous pension so he would persuade the monks to close down their operations. Some of the abbots were also appointed bishops in return for their support. On the other hand, any abbots who refused to cooperate could be charged with treason and sent to prison or executed. Some of the monks were rewarded, too. They were given small amounts of money.

King Henry acquired lands worth many millions of dollars, but he sold off most of them to his supporters for far more. Thus, he succeeded in enriching his treasury at the expense of the monasteries.

New Religious Doctrines

So far, the English Reformation had been largely a political change. The king had achieved power over the Church and had enriched his treasury at the expense of the monasteries. But King Henry VIII probably did not really want to change the religious beliefs of the English people very drastically. He still believed in most of the doctrines of the Catholic Church. Archbishop Cranmer and Thomas Cromwell, however, wanted to move the religion of England closer to the Protestant beliefs of Martin Luther. They were opposed by more Catholic-leaning bishops who agreed with the religious position of King Henry.

In 1536, as the monasteries were being dissolved, the English bishops introduced a series of new religious doctrines that were called the Ten Articles. These represented a compromise. On one side were the Catholic-leaning bishops, such as Stephen Gardiner, bishop of Winchester. On the other side were men such as Archbishop Cranmer, who wanted more Protestant reforms. Although these more radical bishops were outnumbered, they had the strong support of the powerful Thomas Cromwell.

According to the compromise of the Ten Articles, the seven sacraments of the Catholic Church were now reduced to three. These included baptism, holy communion, and confession. In addition to this change, every English church was also required to have a Bible written in English, not Latin. In Germany, Martin Luther had translated the Bible into German, instead of Latin, so it could be read by the common people, instead of only by the well educated clergy. This reform took much power out of the hands of the clergy. Common people could now have more

Thomas Cranmer, as Archbishop of Canterbury, played a pivotal role in Henry VIII's break with the Roman Church.

direct contact with God by reading the passages in the Bible themselves.

The Pilgrimage of Grace

While the king was pursuing his reform of the English Church, discontent was growing among his subjects. Some of them believed that the Church reforms had already gone too far and that religious leaders like Thomas Cranmer should be removed.

The people also resented the growing power of Thomas Cromwell. Additionally, in the north of England, the monasteries had served the needs of the poor far more effectively than in other parts of the realm. In these areas, there was strong resentment against the king for dissolving them.

In early October 1536, revolts broke out north of London. An army of thirty thousand men formed in Lincolnshire. They not only opposed the king's religious reforms but also the new taxes he was trying to raise. At one abbey, the monks armed themselves. With the support of local townspeople, they refused to close down.[6]

The king sent an army north to deal with the rebels, but it was far too small to defeat all of them. Finally, the rebels decided to end their revolt when the king agreed to grant every man involved a pardon and not put him in prison. The rebels had never planned to try to overthrow the king. They just wanted him to roll back his reforms. Although Henry seemed to agree to listen to the rebel demands, he never actually planned to make any of the changes the rebels wanted.

Meanwhile, another revolt had broken out in Yorkshire, in the north of England. Led by a local attorney named Robert Aske, it was called the Pilgrimage of Grace. As they marched, these rebels sang:

> *Christ crucified*
> *For thy wounds wide*
> *Us commons guide*
> *Which pilgrims be,*
> *Through God's grace*
> *For to purchase*
> *Old wealth and peace . . .*[7]

Once again, the king sent his armies to confront the rebels. But again the rebels far outnumbered the royal forces. Some of the men who joined Aske wanted to march on London, where there was very little defense to stop them. But Aske, who was a loyal subject of the king, refused. When Henry pardoned all Aske's men and agreed to hold a special Parliament to deal with their grievances, Aske persuaded his followers to put down their weapons. Then he went to London at the invitation of the king.

Over the winter, however, more revolts broke out. Peasants tried to seize the towns of Hull and Scarborough in northern England and laid siege to Carlisle in the north. Robert Aske called on these men to stop fighting. Meanwhile, King Henry sent a stronger army northward and captured many of the peasants. This time, he dealt with them harshly, hanging some of them as punishment for their role in the rebellion. Then Henry arrested Aske and executed him.

In 1537, Thomas Cromwell established a Council of the North. It would rule over the northern part of England and report directly to the king. This signified the increasing power of the monarchy. In the past, powerful lords had controlled the northern counties. But they had proven incapable of putting down the recent revolts, which had continued until the king sent his own armies northward.

A Male Heir and a New Queen

On October 12, 1537, Jane Seymour gave birth to a son. He was named Edward. Finally, the king had his long-awaited male heir. His dynasty was secure. Unfortunately, twelve days later, Queen Jane died of complications from childbirth. Henry mourned her loss deeply. "Divine Providence hath mingled my joy with the bitterness of the death of her who brought me this happiness," he said.[8]

Although the king now had a male heir, he still faced other problems. In 1538, the pope issued a bull, or directive. The pope declared that Henry was no longer king of England and that his subjects should not obey him. He urged the Catholic monarchs of Europe to attack and destroy the king of England. Henry called out the militia and strengthened the country's coastal defenses in case of invasion. But none ever came. In Germany, many Catholics had become Protestant followers of Martin Luther. The Holy Roman emperor, Charles V, was far too involved with putting down Protestant revolts in Germany to mount an invasion of England.

Nevertheless, King Henry realized that he might need an ally on the European continent. Since he was once more without a wife, he decided to select someone who might help him improve his relations with the Protestant princes of Europe. In Germany, the Duke of Cleves was allied with other Protestant leaders against Emperor Charles V. Henry began to focus his attentions on the duke's daughters, Anne and Amelia. The king sent his court painter, Hans Holbein, to Cleves. Holbein was told to paint portraits of both sisters and bring them back to Henry so he could chose the one who pleased him.

When Holbein returned to England with the portraits, Henry decided that Anne was more attractive to him. Apparently, however, the court painter had produced a very flattering picture of Anne that was far different from how she looked in person. When she finally arrived in England late in 1539 and King Henry saw her, he was extremely disappointed.

The king wanted to break his agreement to marry Anne. He said to Cromwell, who had helped arrange the marriage, "Is there none other remedy but that I must need against my will put my neck in the yoke?"[9] But Cromwell assured the king that he had to go through with the marriage.

Henry VIII was disappointed to find Anne of Cleves not as beautiful as he had expected after seeing her portrait (seen here).

The Fall of Cromwell

For ten years, Thomas Cromwell had been the chief engineer of King Henry's reforms. During that period, the king had tried to establish a middle road between Protestantism and Catholicism. In 1539, he believed that the reforms had gone far enough. Most of the tenets of Catholicism had been retained. For example, Henry strongly believed that the body and blood of Jesus Christ were actually present in the bread and wine of communion. The Lutherans—followers of Martin Luther—on the other hand, believed that communion only symbolized the body and blood of Christ. In addition, while the Lutherans allowed their priests to marry, Henry forbade it, believing priests should remain celibate. Nevertheless, the king, not the pope, remained head of the Church of England.

Thomas Cromwell probably would have liked to have gone further down the road of reform. But he was quickly losing the support of the king. Henry never forgave Cromwell for arranging the marriage with Anne of Cleves. Several months after the marriage, Henry divorced her. He gave her substantial lands, spacious homes, and an income. They remained friendly, even after the divorce.

Meanwhile, Cromwell's enemies sensed that the time had come when they might remove him. Since he had been so powerful for so long, Cromwell, like Wolsey before him, had been envied by some of the great nobles in England. He had also engineered the downfall of many people who had opposed him.

Finally, some of the aristocrats convinced Henry that Cromwell did not have the king's interests at heart. Henry believed them, because he was already angry at Cromwell for arranging his marriage to Anne of Cleves.

Cromwell was arrested and beheaded on July 28, 1540. On the same day, King Henry married again. His new wife was Catherine Howard, the twenty-year-old niece of the powerful Duke of Norfolk. The king was more than twice her age, and by now, he had grown extremely fat. One suit of armor he wore measured fifty-four inches at the waist.[10]

Henry was married to Catherine for only a short time before he discovered that she had been carrying on affairs with several men before their marriage. Indeed, she was believed to be still having a relation-

ship with one of them even after she married the king. Henry was appalled and humiliated. He decided that Catherine should pay dearly for her indiscretions. The young queen

Catherine Howard was married to Henry VIII for just a short time before she was accused of adultery and put to death.

was arrested, found guilty of adultery, and beheaded in 1542.

A year later, Henry took his sixth and last wife, thirty-one-year-old Catherine Parr. She had already been widowed twice. She would outlive the king.

The Final Years

During the last years of his reign, Henry tried to solidify the reforms he had brought to England and maintain the new English, or Anglican, Church. The Church was essentially Catholic in its doctrines, but it was "divorced from Rome as a body of Christians."[11] On one side, the pro-Catholic bishops wanted to return the English Church to the control of Rome. On the other side, bishops such as Thomas Cranmer wanted to go further toward Protestantism. The king, however, seemed content to keep an uneasy balance between both factions.

Some heretics (non-believers) who did not support the king but veered too far toward Catholicism or Protestantism were burned at the stake or hanged. During Henry's reign, however, there were very few executions for heresy. When several powerful bishops led by Stephen Gardiner wanted to arrest Archbishop Cranmer for wanting to make too many changes in the Church, Henry came to his defense. The night before he was due to be seized, Henry summoned Cranmer and assured himself of the bishop's loyalty. Then he gave Cranmer a royal ring. The following day, when he was arrested, Cranmer simply produced the ring,

Catherine Parr was the last of Henry VIII's six wives. A learned woman, she would outlive the king.

showing his enemies that he was under the protection of the king. The crisis passed.

In 1546, a plot developed to send Catherine Parr to prison. She was a Protestant and was disliked by some of the Catholic bishops. Once again, Henry stepped in and saved his wife from arrest.

In January 1547, at age fifty-six, King Henry VIII died. He left behind an English Reformation that was essentially a compromise. Many of his powerful subjects on both sides of the religious debate were not happy with what he had accomplished. They would continue their battle during the reign of Henry's son, nine-year-old Edward VI.

Chapter 8

The King's Legacy

Henry VIII led the English Reformation along the course he had set for it. He established the English, or Anglican, Church, which remains the most powerful church in England today. The king brought an end to the power of the pope over the Church in England, making himself the head of the Church. Henry, not the pope, appointed bishops. The king also ended the centuries-old tradition of providing financial support to Rome. This money remained in England.

Many of the English people supported Henry for doing these things because they had little love for the pope or the Catholic clergy. They applauded their king, who was powerful enough to defy the pope and assert the independence of England. The English, however, were less happy about the king's personal life. Henry's reforms enabled him to marry six times,

King Henry VIII is known today as one of the greatest rulers in English history.

and on two occasions, to brutally execute his wives. But, in part, his numerous marriages arose out of his desire to have a son. A male heir seemed essential to protect the Tudor dynasty on the throne of England and to preserve peace throughout the realm.

The Reformation in England was primarily a political change. That is, more power was concentrated in the hands of the king. Henry shared some of this power with Parliament, which participated in approving all the legislation that made the English Reformation possible.

In religious doctrines, there were fewer changes. Henry did not support many of the new religious beliefs that formed a part of Lutheranism. Unlike Martin Luther, Henry believed that priests should not marry. He was convinced that the body and blood of Christ were actually present in the sacrament of communion, not that it was only a symbol of Christ's suffering. He also thought that a person's soul would be saved by a combination of faith and good works, not faith alone, as Lutherans believed.

But in other areas, Henry moved the English Church closer to Protestantism. For example, the Bible was now translated into English, a language of the common people. The same thing had happened on the European continent where Martin Luther had translated the Bible into German. Henry reduced the wealth of the Church and the power of the clergy by eliminating the monasteries. The writings of Luther and other Protestant leaders were now being imported into England. Henry had also proven himself a friend to English bishops, like Thomas Cranmer, who wanted to move the English Reformation further down the road toward Protestantism.

Henry had produced a compromise to suit his own needs. With his powerful personality, Henry made sure that no one would defy him—at least, not for long. Heretics who disagreed with the king might pay for it by being burned at the stake. But the compromise lasted only as long as Henry was king. After his death, there would be more changes.

The Reign of Edward VI and "Bloody" Mary

Edward was only a boy when he became king. But he was a devout child who believed in many of the Protestant religious doctrines. He was also surrounded by powerful advisors who wanted to continue the English Reformation. Among these advisors was his uncle Edward Seymour, Earl of Hertford. Because Edward was a minor, the earl ruled for him as "Protector of all the realms and dominions of the King's majesty . . . and . . . Governor of his most royal person."[1]

In 1549, a new law was passed by Parliament, which allowed the clergy to marry. A new prayer book was introduced, including only Protestant prayers. Several years later, the Act of Uniformity required that all the king's subjects must attend services of the Anglican Church. King Henry's compromise had been broken. Among England's leaders, Protestantism had taken a much firmer hold. But among the lower levels of society, many of the old Catholic beliefs still remained. It would take many more years of Edward's leadership before real change occurred.

However, the new king would not be given this time. He died in 1553 of tuberculosis. Edward was succeeded by his half sister Mary, the daughter of Catherine of Aragon. (Before his death, Henry had recognized Mary as one of his heirs, although she had earlier been made illegitimate by the king's marriage to Anne Boleyn.) Mary had decided that England must return to Catholicism, and she had the full support of her cousin, Holy Roman Emperor Charles V.

Charles arranged a marriage between Mary and his son, Philip of Spain. The marriage was strongly opposed by many of the English people who cried: "We will have no foreigner for our King."[2] Uprisings took place in various parts of the country to protest Philip's visit to England. Mary's soldiers successfully put down the revolts. The queen had fallen in love with Philip and was resolved to marry him, regardless of what her subjects wanted. Philip, who was eleven years younger than the English queen, felt little affection for her. He agreed to marry her mainly to assure the triumph of Catholicism in England.

In 1554, the same year that Mary and Philip were married, the power of the Catholic Church was restored in England. The wealthy aristocrats were assured that the lands they had received during the breakup of the monasteries would not be taken away. Therefore, they were prepared to support Mary when she recognized the authority of the pope. The Act of Supremacy, passed during the reign of Henry VIII, was repealed. All the religious changes that occurred under Henry and his son, Edward, were also removed. England returned to Catholicism.

But Mary's religious revolution proved to be far more difficult than she might have believed. Some of the English people did not want to change their beliefs. Among them was Archbishop Thomas Cranmer. When he refused to support Mary, Cranmer was burned at the stake as a heretic. Almost three hundred other people also lost their lives during

Mary's reign. One woman gave birth to a baby as she was being burned. The newborn was thrown into the fire with her.[3]

For her brutal reign of terror, the queen was called "Bloody Mary" by Protestants. In her effort

Edward VI, Henry's only male heir, died at the age of fifteen, leaving England, as King Henry VIII had feared, in the hands of his half sister Mary.

to restore Catholicism, Mary had gone too far. For centuries after her death, the English people would regard Catholicism as a "cruel and persecuting religion."[4] They would not want to see it restored. When Mary died in 1558 after a short reign, her policies died with her. She did not produce an heir to carry on her plan.

Elizabeth I

Mary's Catholic advisors had wanted her to prevent her half sister Elizabeth from ever becoming queen. The daughter of Anne Boleyn, Elizabeth was next in line for the throne. Elizabeth supported the religious reforms of her father. The Succession Act had recognized Elizabeth as a legitimate daughter of Henry VIII, and therefore, she had the right eventually to succeed him. Mary had hated Elizabeth for her beliefs, but she was not cruel enough to execute her, as Elizabeth feared.

In 1558, after Mary's death, Elizabeth became queen of England. She rapidly began to roll back the Catholic reforms of her sister's reign. Once again, the monarch became head of the Church of England. She accepted the new prayer book that had been written during the reign of Edward VI. Reading the English Bible was encouraged throughout her realm. While some of her Protestant subjects wanted the queen to go farther, she refused. Elizabeth also refrained from persecuting Protestant or Catholic heretics who did not support the Church of England.

Queen Elizabeth continued her father's reforms, making herself head of the Anglican Church.

Like her father, Elizabeth charted a middle course in matters of religion. During her long reign of more than forty years, the queen succeeded in establishing the Church of England as a sturdy institution that would survive long after her death. England became a bulwark of Protestantism. In 1588, Philip of Spain launched a great fleet, called the Spanish Armada, to invade England and try to convert it to Catholicism. The Armada was defeated by an English fleet. Elizabeth and England retained their independence and their Protestant religion.

Queen Elizabeth I had carried out the religious goals of her father. Today, the Anglican Church that Henry VIII started remains the religion of a large majority of the English people, with the monarch of England at its head.

Timeline

1399—Richard II overthrown, beginning a century of English political turmoil; Henry IV becomes king and begins the Lancastrian dynasty.

1413—Henry IV dies.

1415—Henry V wins the decisive Battle of Agincourt.

1422—Henry V dies.

1453—Henry VI goes temporarily insane.

1455—War of the Roses begins.

1461—Edward IV becomes king and House of York is supreme in England.

1470—Henry VI recaptures the throne of England.

1471—Edward IV defeats Henry and brings stable government to the realm.

1483—Edward IV dies; His son reigns briefly as Edward V before Edward IV's brother Richard III usurps the throne.

1485—Richard III is overthrown by Henry Tudor at Bosworth Field; Henry Tudor rules as Henry VII and marries Elizabeth of York.

1486—Arthur is born to Henry and Elizabeth.

1492—Henry is born to Henry and Elizabeth.

1502—Arthur dies from serious illness; Henry becomes heir to the throne.

1509—Henry VIII becomes king; He marries his brother's widow, Catherine of Aragon.

1513—Henry invades France.

1516—Mary Tudor is born to King Henry and Queen Catherine.

1517—Martin Luther begins Protestant Reformation in Germany.

1518—Henry and Francis I of France meet at the Field of the Cloth of Gold.

1521—Henry publishes *The Defense of the Seven Sacraments.*

1529—Fall of Cardinal Thomas Wolsey as the king's chief minister.

1532—Parliament passes the Submission of the Clergy; Parliament passes the Act of Annates.

1533—Parliament passes the Act in Restraint of Appeals; Henry secretly marries Anne Boleyn; Henry's marriage to Catherine is declared dissolved; Elizabeth, the future queen, is born to Anne and Henry.

1534—Parliament passes the Succession Act; Parliament passes the Act of Supremacy; Church of England is established.

1535—John Fisher and Sir Thomas More are executed.

1536—Anne Boleyn is executed; Henry marries Jane Seymour; Henry and Thomas Cromwell dissolve the monasteries; Pilgrimage of Grace begins.

1537—Jane Seymour gives birth to a son, the future Edward VI, then she dies.

1540—Henry marries Anne of Cleves; He divorces her a few months later; Thomas Cromwell is executed; Henry marries Catherine Howard.

1542—Catherine Howard is executed.

1543—Henry marries Catherine Parr.

1547—Henry dies; Edward VI becomes king.

1552—Parliament passes the Act of Uniformity; Protestantism takes firmer hold.

1553—Edward VI dies; Mary becomes queen.

1554—Mary marries Philip of Spain; She restores England to Catholicism.

1558—Mary dies; Elizabeth I becomes queen; Elizabeth begins restoring the Church of England.

1588—Defeat of Spanish Armada preserves England and safeguards Protestantism in the realm.

Chapter Notes

Chapter 2. England in Turmoil

1. William Shakespeare, "King Richard II," Act III, Scene III, *The Complete Works of William Shakespeare* (New York: Cumberland Publishing Company, 1911), p. 456.

2. A. L. Rowse, *Bosworth Field* (Garden City, N.Y.: Doubleday, 1966), p. 70.

3. William Shakespeare, "King Richard III," Act V, Scene IV, *The Complete Works of William Shakespeare* (New York: Cumberland Publishing Company, 1911), p. 731.

4. Rowse, p. 127.

5. Frank Arthur Mumby, *The Youth of Henry VIII* (Boston: Houghton Mifflin, 1913), p. 3.

6. Carolly Erickson, *Great Harry* (New York: Summit Books, 1980), p. 44.

Chapter 3. The Young King

1. J. J. Scarisbrick, *Henry VIII* (Berkeley: University of California, 1968), p. 13.

2. Carolly Erickson, *Great Harry* (New York: Summit Books, 1980), pp. 54–55.

3. Jackson J. Spielvogel, *Western Civilization*, 4th ed. (Belmont, Calif.: Thomson Learning, 1999), p. 365.

4. James Anthony Froude, *Life and Letters of Erasmus* (London: Longmans, 1895), p. 98.

Chapter 4. The Reformation Begins

1. Martin Luther, "Martin Luther Protests Against the Sale of Indulgences, Wittenberg, Germany, 1517," *The Mammoth Book of Eyewitness History*, ed. Jon E. Lewis (New York: Carroll & Graf Publishers, Inc., 1998), pp. 103–104.

Chapter 5. Henry's Marriage Crisis

1. Antonia Fraser, *The Wives of Henry VIII* (New York: Knopf, 1992), pp. 129–130.

2. Anniina Joniken, "Henry VIII to Anne Boleyn," *Renaissance Literature*, 1996–2000, <http://www.luminarium.org/renlit/henrytoanne.htm> (January 22, 2001).

3. Fraser, p. 137.

4. Carolly Erickson, *Great Harry* (New York: Summit Books, 1980), p. 209.

5. Fraser, p. 150.

6. Eric Ives, *Anne Boleyn* (Oxford: Basil Blackwell, 1986), p. 140.

7. Fraser, p. 160.

Chapter 6. Henry Launches a Reformation

1. G. R. Elton, ed., *The New Cambridge Modern History, Volume II, The Reformation, 1520–1559* (Cambridge: Cambridge University Press, 1958), p. 226.

2. Peter Ackroyd, *The Life of Thomas More* (New York: Doubleday, 1998), p. 319.

3. Ibid.

4. Ibid., p. 284.

5. Robert Lacey, *The Life and Times of Henry VIII* (New York: Praeger, 1974), p. 122.

6. Paul Halsall, "Modern History Sourcebook: Sir Thomas More, *Utopia*, 1516," *Modern History Sourcebook*, 1997, <http://www.fordham.edu/halsall/mod/thomasmore-utopia.html> (January 22, 2001).

7. A. G. Dickens, *Thomas Cromwell and the English Reformation*, Rev. ed. (London: The English Universities Press, 1967), p. 55.

8. Ackroyd, p. 361.

9. Milton Viorst, ed., *The Great Documents of Western Civilization* (New York: Barnes and Noble, 1965), pp. 97–98.

10. Lacey, p. 146.

Chapter 7. Henry's Realm in Turmoil

1. Retha Warnicke, *The Rise and Fall of Anne Boleyn* (New York: Cambridge University Press, 1989), p. 199.

2. Antonia Fraser, *The Wives of Henry VIII* (New York: Knopf, 1992), p. 236.

3. Robert Lacey, *The Life and Times of Henry VIII* (New York: Praeger, 1972), pp. 155–156.

4. John Carey, ed., "The Progress of the English Reformation, 1537–8: Cromwell's Agents' Report," *Eyewitness to History* (New York: Avon Books, 1987), pp. 89–90.

5. Jasper Ridley, *Henry VIII* (New York: Viking, 1984), p. 256.

6. Ibid., p. 285.

7. Ibid., p. 287.

8. Lacey, p. 168.

9. Ridley, p. 335.

10. Ibid., p. 348.

11. G. R. Elton, ed., *The New Cambridge Modern History, Volume II, The Reformation, 1520–1559* (Cambridge: Cambridge University Press, 1958), p. 241.

Chapter 8. The King's Legacy

1. Alison Plowden, *The House of Tudor* (New York: Stein and Day, 1976), p. 126.

2. Ibid., p. 168.

3. Jane Resh Thomas, *Behind the Mask: The Life of Queen Elizabeth I* (New York: Clarion Books, 1998), p. 72.

4. G. R. Elton, ed., *The New Cambridge Modern History, Volume II, The Reformation, 1520–1559* (Cambridge: Cambridge University Press, 1958), p. 248.

Further Reading and Internet Addresses

Books

Dwyer, Frank. *Henry VIII*. Broomall, Pa.: Chelsea House Publishers, 1988.

Erickson, Carolly. *Great Harry*. New York: Summit Books, 1980.

Fraser, Antonia. *The Wives of Henry VIII*. New York: Knopf, 1992.

Ives, Eric. *Anne Boleyn*. Oxford: Basil Blackwell, 1986.

Ridley, Jasper. *Henry VIII*. New York: Viking Press, 1984.

Thomas, Jane. *Behind The Mask: The Life of Queen Elizabeth I*. New York: Clarion Books, 1998.

Turner, Dorothy. *Henry VIII*. New York: Franklin Watts, 1988.

Internet Addresses

Britannia. *Henry VIII (1509–47 AD)*. 2000. <http://www.britannia.com/history/monarchs/mon41.html>.

Henry the Eighth. n.d. <http://www.englishhistory.net/tudor/monarchs/henry8.html>.

Hooker, Richard. "Discovery and Reformation." *World Civilizations*. 1996. <http://www.wsu.edu/~dee/REFORM/ENGLAND.HTM>.

Jokinen, Anniina. "Henry VIII, 1491–1547." *Renaissance English Literature*. 1996–2000. <http://www.luminarium.org/renlit/tudor.htm>.

Index